A GLADIATOR'S JOURNEY

BRIAN COATES

authorHOUSE°

AuthorHouse™
1663 Liberty Drive
Bloomington, IN 47403
www.authorhouse.com
Phone: 1 (800) 839-8640

Published by AuthorHouse 12/13/2017

ISBN: 978-1-5462-1619-3 (sc)
ISBN: 978-1-5462-1618-6 (hc)
ISBN: 978-1-5462-1617-9 (e)

Library of Congress Control Number: 2017917132

Print information available on the last page.

This book is printed on acid-free paper.

CONTENTS

Hope Emerges

Under the Armor

His Purpleness

Imagine you as a child, running, playing, and hunting with your friends and elders in the African Savannah. Suddenly and without warning, you are captured, put on a boat, and whisked away across unknown waters. After what seems like an eternity, you land in a new place with only those that survived the trip with you. During this trip, you have witnessed and/or been a part of ungodly savagery, beat until your skin breaks open which was made worse by the sting of the salt water, deprived of sunlight by being chained in the hold of the ship, "living" in squalor like you have never seen before, perhaps defecating on yourself-unable to clean up and observing sickness and death all around you. You come to this new land only to be kept chained, split from those with whom you are familiar, sold like cattle, and made to stay on a land due to fear of being beaten and/or lynched. You have to endure the most basic of abodes and eating the scraps of your captors. Unbeknownst to you is that you have now entered your first "hood" and this is the set you are now claiming, setting the stage of hood claiming for decades to come. Every now and then someone does escape. However, those that do get away oftentimes return severely beaten and/or put to death right in front of you.

These, and similar or worse, scenarios playout in many different cultures (i.e., Holocaust, Japanese internment, etc.) and in many different decades, yet the outcome is the same. Your choices have been limited because fear of reprisal. This creates allostatic load (stress) inside your lineage (your grandparents, great grandparents, etc.) for which you have no help/relief.

Allostatic load is defined as "the wear and tear on the body" which accumulates as an individual is exposed to repeated or chronic stress. It represents the physiological consequences of chronic exposure to fluctuating or heightened neural or neuroendocrine response that results from repeated or chronic stress

This allostatic stress can be passed down generationally without the current recipient even knowing. There is thought that allostatic stress is a major factor in low birthrate babies, and it could also factor into generational alcoholism, generational eating habits and chronic illnesses such as diabetes, etc.

Today, a baby is born. Parents the world over imagine the possibilities for this new life. What this new person can do and how far they can go. In effect, this new parent is imagining the choices that this child will have and hope that those choices are many more than the parent had. What the parent doesn't know is that they, the parent, will contribute to the dwindling of this child's choices for years to come. Every time the parent fails to meet the needs of this child, a choice is lost. Every time the parent yells, speaks ill of, spanks, belittles, etc., this child's world has gotten smaller. Each time you fail to venture out to meet new people, explore new things, and take on new responsibilities, this child's world just got smaller. In addition to all the things that have to be navigated throughout their lifetime, if the parent is unavailable to help navigate, their world has been reduced to nothing.

The journey that you are about to embark is one of pain, confusion, recovery and healing. This story, told in a series of poems, will induce tears of sadness, provoke anger, instill fear, but will ultimately bring you strength, hope and joy.

The poems will take you on an adventure of a little boy's journey into manhood as he is molded into a gladiator by limited choices, isolation, racism, and alcoholism. This story will culminate into the adult child finally seeing the error in his ways, the pain he has caused, and ultimately recognizing what has contributed to his life choices, philosophies, etc. It will take you into an abyss of pain that he has had to endure, recognition and recovery from that pain, and a healing that provides glimpses of what can be and what is out there for him. It does not matter his age, as there is still plenty of life for him to reach for and life for him to live. He still has time to live like he has never been hurt before, and have fun like no one is watching. Remembering that a life half lived is no life at all.

My hope, is to touch people in such a way that encourages them to explore the possibility that they too may have issues entrenched in their past. If this is you, I hope you comprehend that there are resources that will and can help you and that you will seek out the help you need. Adult Children of Alcoholics and other Dysfunctional Families (ACA), Al-Anon, AA, etc., these are all designed for you. If these poems can touch just one life, get just one person into the rooms of recovery they will have completed some service to the community.

Gladiators Pain will detail the development of the warrior after years of abandonment and abuse. It will show the tears that are now shed for a childhood lost, the long term effects of the abandonment, the confusion of being unloved, and the bout of racism that pushed him further into the abyss of pain. Although at times it may appear to be anger, in reality it is masked pain.

A Gladiator Surrenders will display the weariness of the gladiator after years of battle. He is ready and willing to put down his sword and accept the crushing blow of defeat. The Gladiator recognizes that there is and has always been a higher power guiding him, and has now brought him to a new reality. With this higher powers guidance, there is hope and recovery around the corner.

Hope Emerges shows that once the Gladiator has laid down his sword, there is no going back. He is beginning to get in touch with emotions other than anger and is being re-built after being torn to the core.

Under the Armor displays the friendliness, playfulness and observations that the Gladiator can have. The Gladiator is beginning to have lightness in his life.

His Purpleness – When you get there, this will be self-explanatory

While contemplating these poems, keep in mind that they were not conceived or written on a linear trajectory, the warrior is still healing.

With healing comes the peeling of the onion that could reveal even more pain and more recovery. This warrior will continue to recognize and write about the lightness in his life and continue to enjoy this new found freedom as he moves further and further away from being in the fighting pit.

God, grant me the serenity to accept the things that I cannot change,
The courage to change the things I can
And the wisdom to know the difference.

A Gladiators Pain

I HAVE BEEN FIGHTING
SINCE I WAS A CHILD
I'M NOT A SURVIVOR
I'M A FUCKING WARRIOR

SHATTERED

The crack of the whip began at a tender age
Ensuing years bore attempts to corner and cage
In the quest to pursue some other kind
You are not enough my mind would opine
The resiliency was solid through this adversity I faced
The protection of armor as I walked through the place
Although the fight was valiant, I have been broken at last
No more arrows to fire and no more rocks to cast
I no longer answer to Kunta Kinte, to this I vow
As I hang from the gallows, call me Toby now
Like Leonidas, in defeat I lay down my shield
Revealing my underbelly of which I now yield
For the definitive fatal blow for you to give
And then rip it right out of me as I can no longer live
I have been beaten into submission and I can take no more
Only God knows now what lies in store
The weakness is now exposed for you to see
I need you to express this last breath out of me
For it pains me to be this broken man
Please, I beg of you, make it as quick as you can

You Never Asked

Did you know the racism that I encountered
when I was five confused me?
Did you ask how it made me feel and try to help me understand?
Did you know I was afraid to walk to kindergarten alone?
Did you ask if I was ok with walking along that busy street?
Did you know there was someone's big brother
threatening to beat me up in first grade?
Did you ask how my day, week or year was going?
Did you know I watched a kid my age get run over by a car?
Did you ask if I had a good time at my friends house?
Did you know I was afraid of being bussed over to a new school?
Did you ask how the new school was or felt
compelled to help ease my transition?
Did you know I was afraid to fight but had to pretend
I was not scared so people would leave me alone?
Did you ask the reasons behind me fighting at school?
Did you know I had to practice my "meanness"
in order to survive my existence?
Did you ask why or see the shift?
Did you know I really wanted to play organized football?
Did you ask if there were any other sports I
was interested in besides baseball?
Did you Know I would have loved to be in
a spelling bee or debate team?

Did you ask what my interests were or recognize my intelligence?
Did you know I absolutely hated when you chose not to
pick me up at the babysitter after you said you would?
Did you ask how I felt or see/feel my anxiety?
Did you know that I hated the East Sac house as they were mean?
Did you ask why I didn't really like to go over there?
Did you know because of them I stopped crying and started hating?
Did you ask what was going on with me and/or not see the shift?
Did you know I was afraid of moving to a new city?
Did you ask how I was adjusting and/or making friends?
Did you know one main reason of moving back to Sacramento
is I was tired of being called a nigger and not feeling safe?
Did you ask why I wanted to leave?
Did you know that because of this upheaval,
change has since scared me?
Did you ask how I felt about all the change at once?
Did you know when you locked us in that house in
Compton I was afraid I couldn't get out if needed?
Did you ask for my input?
Did you know in Jr. High school I was a
starter on the basketball team?
Did you ask how the season was going or when the games were?
Did you know that I faced a shit storm of racism
in high school surrounding dating?
Did you ask if there were any problems or
recognize that I was never at their house?
Since you didn't ask how my high school dating situation was
You didn't know to ask why I would marry into the same situation
Did you know I was a very good high school football player?
Did you ask how I was doing?
Did you know when I left for college that I
did not know if I had a place to live?
Did you ask if everything was covered?
Because you never asked, I felt like I was not
good enough to protect or love
Why didn't you ever ask?

TODAY I CRY

I cried today
Remembering all those times that I could
have been shown that I mattered
I cried today
Remembering with horror all those who molded me into a gladiator
I cried today
Remembering with grief those that could have shown some tenderness
I cried today
Remembering with contempt those that could have
waited to pass judgement until they met me
I cried today
Remembering as the light of my smile dimmed
For I was a just a boy that had dreams and goals
A boy that wished to grow up and participate in the American Dream
Family, wife, children, good schools and good neighborhood
A boy that yearned to be shown what love and family look like
A boy, afraid to reach out for help, but wanted desperately not to be
Empty remains the yearning
Today I just cry

COMPASSIONATE ENGAGEMENT

Malignancy of the lungs for which he died
A disease from which no one can hide
A lifelong indulger he was for sure
In the end, compassion could have been the cure
This was a malady that would assuredly end the days
Where was the empathy for his wayward ways
Encouragement to seek help is what one would need
Not a separation because of the alcoholic deed
Himself he could not even assist
But the out world you just could not resist
Detachment with love ultimately is what one should do
But to the kids it looked like the coop you flew
Obliterating psyches in your wake
For everyone's feelings did you forsake
As you wear a veil over your love you do mete
Connection with others is a practice of defeat
As you sit in judgement from the perch above
Your approvals were needed for a hint of love
Recall that an unclean bathroom brought rebuke that was swift
As did a damaged child's actions were deemed amiss
Are these acts of compassion, i think not
The rules of engagement have been rethought.

I WAS JUST A BOY

Living the life of Riley and Stand by Me
I was a happy and determined child filled with glee
The world was my oyster I was made to feel
But soon I would discover that this was unreal
Driving cross country to the Carolinas at the end.
Then smacked with racism as soon as we turned the bend
Not understanding because everything was within my reach
But apparently there was so much more to teach
Back to Cali, where everything in sight was agog
Soon forgetting the experience like the burning off of the fog
Junior and Senior High school in Sac were a blast
Creating memories that were surely meant to last
But alas, the ugly head of racism did come back a trace
Unfortunately these are memories that cannot be erased
I believed the Constitution that said all people were created equal
But as the Carolina experience, Listen to the sequel
Our time together produced a very tender and innocent love
But the hue of my skin was rebuffed from above
I initially felt we were in rhythm and rhyme
But in no uncertain terms it was conveyed, not in this lifetime
This reality crushed my spirit and it decimated my soul
Now, as then, I am still not completely whole
On the brink of greatness with tremendous goals and dreams
Now, a shattered shell of who I should be it seems

Unable to fully experience the passages of rites
Puppy love, family dynamics and the view of different sights
Instead, I experienced covert ops, and downright shame
When I should have been experiencing love in full flame
How could you do that to another human being
Did you not have faith in her and as an extension, your teaching?
The collateral damage has taken its toll
Numerous innocents are now broken and old
If you would have only allowed yourself to see
Her love made me such a better person to be
It gave me faith in an otherwise chaotic place
But ultimately I was crushed as you didn't allow the race
I was a child of God just like your daughter you see
I was just a boy, why would you do that to me

THE SCENE OF THE CRIME

The havoc that was wreaked could today put you in a cage
How is this still a thing in this day and age
Why was I unlucky enough to be in a situation so mean
Introduced to the perpetrators of this crime scene
The crime so horrendous that my foundation was rocked
My soul was taken and permanence was out locked
My innocence was stolen and out of sheer relief
If truth be told so was my belief
They say love like you have never been hurt before
But have they ever been shamed and cut to their core
I had love in my heart where now I have none
How can this loss of innocence ever be undone
Holding me together, this love, back then
After this massacre I was as empty as tin man
The words and deeds being displayed I could no longer trust
I could now only rely on my anger and my lust
The many innocent bystanders that were caught in the wake
To think about it now makes my head just shake
Love, what is that, it is nothing real to me
The emptiness in my eyes is what all now see
The scene of the crime to now return
Reintroduction to this hell is where I will eternally burn
I wanted to live out loud and not be forbidden
But everything now has forever been hidden

No one understands my pain or unites in my joy
Hell I lost all knowledge of that as a boy
My intelligence no one even understands
I really crave to be that reverent man
I am starting to understand in order to depart this space
I must have forgiveness in my heart to take its place
To be released from the clutches of hell so dire
To get there though I will have to walk through fire
Faith is all that I have of the flame to douse
To usher the crime scene from this house

Anger Was My Shield

Seething, slow burn, fuming are all different names
They all resemble anger as it burst into flames
Batman had the Batmobile and his armor to adorn
Superman had a cape that shielded his form
My protection was called anger and it never failed me
Like the legendary Leonidas and his 300 mighty
Battle ready was I always to get down in the mix
Unequipped you come, you better rethink this
Because if you dared to confront me ready you think
I would make an example of you quick as a blink
I couldn't understand the viciousness of the attack
I would see red until you reeled all the way back
Then I would satisfy in the carnage presented before me
Didn't matter who it was that lay beneath thee
But the ground that I stood on I would never yield
Because I always knew that anger was my shield

GLADIATOR

It's you against me and why would you dare
You will never survive because I just don't care
My cunning and slyness has helped me befall
I will lure you in and destroy you mind and all
But if it's a physical battle that you rather engage
Oh good lord you can't even fathom the rage
I have been thrown in the pit like a bull for a fight
There is no way for you to win no-no not tonight
As a rooster I will pick your brains and your eyes
I will beat you into submission and tell you bye-bye
And as you tap out, and you will indeed
I will slit your fucking throat as I watch you bleed
I will slash your Achilles and ice pick your knee
I will bite your nuts off if you fuck with me
those that were supposed to love me created this course
Apparently they failed to impart compassion and remorse

PTSD

Wrong is something you could never be
Emotional stifling is what it taught me
Dearly you paid if you dared to be wrong
The remembrance of abuse has been so very long
My body now reacts in ways I do not know
A survival tactic acquired from so long ago
For the tactics have been absorbed and remembered deep
The body now reacts without even a peep
Fear and abandonment is what drives thee
Control of those emotions has eluded me
To be wrong now the endurance of fear has been long
What must people think that I am never wrong
I can feel it in my back, the burden is immense
My abandonment issue is very intense
The pain is dizzying, I can feel it in my shoulders
The knots that have developed are like two ton boulders
Why couldn't the deeds just have been explained to me
Instead of being treated like Kunte Kinte'
I was a mere child curious to explore the ship
But my experience was curtailed by the crack of the whip
I could never share the excitement of what I did today
For fear that it was somehow wrong and I would pay
The tears that now flow are but a fraction of what are
I am still trying to get to all the pain from afar

The outcome was not to share or always be right
No other options existed in my sight
I live in the shadows afraid to share
More afraid than not that most won't care
The loneliness and suffering of always being right
I can no longer engage in the infinite fight
I now surrender for I have finally lost
Time to pay the ultimate cost
So I put down my weapon, I bend my knee
I bow my head and I whisper please take me
This trauma I suffer can no more be
I have nothing else for which to give to thee

A GLADIATOR
SURRENDERS

REST

For years I have envisioned a resting of my head
Closing my eyes and never again rising from the bed
A smooth transition from earth to the pearly gates
Leaving behind the chaos, the fanfare and all those who hate
Aye, as I once wrote, am a gladiator at heart
The struggle has been a result of combat from the start
I have grown weary with all the battles neath my belt
Succumbing to a crushing death is where I found comfort and felt
Though my warrior tendencies would not allow me to fail
But enjoyment of the fruit was oftentimes frail
Battle scars were quite often the outcome of this reign
But they were internal so no one could imagine the pain
Why did I compete for those things I did not fully enjoy
Because they told me to, from the time that I was a boy
It was never communicated to enjoy, only to get
So when I obtained, all I did was push reset
They told me more was better or different was good
But I don't think that they ever really understood
I needed love and compassion to rest my body and my weary brain
Because of this drought I think I might be going insane
Stuffing my feelings and then holding them at bay
My ability to do this because that is the gladiator's way
But I realize now that the battle is being lost
I am suffering immensely and paying the cost

I need time away from all the chaos of life
A retreat is what I seek for solace from this strife
No decisions to make, no soothing of feelings
No control to try to take, just relaxation and healing
Admitting this of course is the ultimate admission
That I cannot handle it alone, the ultimate submission
I am ready to give this and to take the time
But I am afraid of how the outcome will beseech my mind
That is my control speaking as though I still can
Control others ways or lay out a plan
One day at a time is how I now must live
And not concern myself with how this will give
Now is the time for me to start enjoying and more
And the god given talents that I was afraid to explore
That a poem could flow, who would have known
Or that I had desire to create art in other ways I have shown
As I create, I tap into a whole other side
Feelings are exposed when once put aside
Too sensitive I was deemed so many years ago
So the gladiator was created to defeat this foe
To get back to that boy I once was I now strive
Allowing his feelings to show and never to hide
I am so tired of fighting it has taken the life out of me
I must now rest if I am to survive and continue on this journey

RAISING THE WHITE FLAG

In my innocence, all alone I came to believe
No persistent and consistent guidance was provided to me
My vision of the world I could only rely
How that kept my world small and my dreams close by
Hurling aimlessly through existence because I had no rudder
Only dreaming small dreams because there were no other
My way was the only way to produce the desired outcome
Oh how so damaging did this behavior become
I have come to see that you have reached out before
But my education failed me to grasp and explore
I could not recognize that you were trying to assist
All I could see were the adversities destroying the bliss
The ism's of the span that I have had to endure
Molded me into this thing that I absolutely abhor
To now know there is a higher power that carries me across the sand
Gives me comfort and belief that goes way beyond this land
With this teaching how could I now surrender to thee
When it has been a lifetime of trusting only in me
But capitulate I will, on bended knee
I am depending on you that you will care for me
You will nurture the innocent child that is still inside
Support me to grow into the man that I often hide
My yielding will be complete once I relinquish control
Allowing loving out loud, dreaming big dreams and passion to hold

I will love like I have never been hurt before
My smile will be as bold and bright as Sharper's of yore
My heart will openly cry for those in despair
And I will never again utter the words, I don't care.
My nature will be something no one will even remember
Today I start the metamorphosis of my unconditional surrender

SURVIVAL

If you didn't grow up in this lineage how
could you comprehend the span
Survival of a childhood is very difficult to understand
Beatings, abandonment, the emotional toll
Late nights all alone, watching the whirlwind unfold
Waiting and wondering when they will arrive
How does a child get through this and ultimately survive
Navigating through all the confrontations of life
Everything no matter what it is particularly the strife
To figure life's systems presented so much grief
Why couldn't I access at least some adult relief
Having conversations and trying to understand their words
Sharing things with them, not knowing if you have been heard
Not ever knowing when the big scary might show and appear
Either, it didn't matter as they both were to be feared
Fearful to move at times because it seemed
like every action was wrong
Respite of a holiday or gathering is what you would long
For these days offered you at least some safe keep
These are the only times they might hold their tongue and not leap
Christmas was wonderful because you knew there would not be grief
Thanksgiving as well as it too offered relief
Fourth of July was another that delivered a pause
Even Easter was a day that provided for the cause

Is this why I cling to the traditional scope
They no longer really provide, but I do always hope
I continue to look to these days for comfort and joy
As I did during the days of being that scared little boy
But as each year passes it seems further away
From those happy memories tied to each one of those days
I need to release these remembrances and create something a new
For these recollections it's about time I did slew

The Walk

Survival of this journey I have had to endure
Healing of my heart and mind is what I seek to cure
I conferred with my higher power and it was relayed to me
Through all your trials you must trust and I will guide thee
The footprints in the sand were an enduring sight
I tried and tried to believe with all my might
But as I noticed the one set of prints in the sand that I see
I had come to believe that my higher power had forsaken me
Through the sands of time beginning with one grain
I truly believed that I walked alone in this porous rain
How could I be so arrogant and so blind
To even have a belief that those footprints were all mine
I have come to realize that I have walked one step for your every ten
I am not even sure when all this carrying began
Was it at birth before chaos and all
Or was at ten when the earthly family did stall
Maybe it was ELHI when I thought all was known
Potentially after that when I felt I was grown.
What I really needed was to acknowledge and see
That in order to survive I needed help from thee
You guided me to this ACA family that has embraced me so whole
That healing is what I am beginning to feel in my soul
Thank you to my new family for the support and love
For guidance mine eyes will now forever look up above.

TWO BLOWS

I grew up reveling in the world's ebbs and flows
Then I was dealt 2 disturbing and heart wrenching blows
The first was very blatant and right in my face
The other was mysterious and even harder to erase
The first blow called Racism struck me out of nowhere
I couldn't believe that it seemed like folks just didn't care
Didn't really feel it until I traveled away from sactown
Went down to the Deep South where it was present all around
Then on to San Berdoo where it struck me again
Wow, people don't like me because of the color of my skin
The other more devastating punch is alcoholism
It locked me up where I remain still in this prison
With no key to escape or no parole date in sight
Surviving childhood and beyond was the
only thing on this paths flight
It is said, more than you can handle god will not give
But this one two punch is hard to outlive
What about the all the innocents that have had to deal
With uncaring and devastation that was ultimately revealed
To keep my sense of control and order in my life
I had to institute rules to keep down the continuous strife
You could not imagine how devastating or how it makes you reel
To understand that you have only survived and were made not to feel
Self-help is what I always hoped would assist

But Al-Anon and ACA seem to have the tools to persist
By all accounts I do matter is what I must learn
And self-care is what I must internally burn
Right now confusion is what I mostly feel
As I realize that what I have learned thus far is not real
Movies like the Notebook used to make my heart sing
But I am learning this is not realistic as there is conflict in between
I must learn how to navigate and constructively deal
With this in a way that people know that I do feel
Caring and loving and not angry and mad
I want understanding and love not to make people sad
I am a work in progress and I will continue to write
The initiation of healing is definitely in sight

DIVERSIFICATION OF THE MIND

The freedom that is revealed when you realize
That choice is what truly gives you joy in your life
How liberating it has become to now understand
That variety is always right there close at hand
Options are implicit in all interactions that you do
Whether school you go to or career waiting for you
With whom you intertwine is also a choice
You now need to remember that you too have a voice
You have a choice to reject the terms by
those that are supposed to love
You can also opt to, or not, walk with the spirt from above
Upon review, miniscule may be your array sphere of the past
Without understanding you fought for small
alternatives like they were your last
Rage from all this is what I would call the protection modality
Your protector now offers peace as your new true reality
No longer toward you inferior attitudes do you have to accept thus
You no longer need to interact with those that appear to hate us.
Although you survived childhood you now have a choice to live
You no longer have to accept what others are willing to give

SHACKLES

Options were limited the moment we embarked the ships
Plantation owners solidified these limitations with bullwhips
Today we are still bound by laying claim to our hood
The shackles of our mind today must be understood
We learned to be subjugated by the beatings we took
This provided the vessel to continue the enslavement to cook
Allostatic stress is the imprisonment of the treatment from so long ago
The funny thing is that the punishment of the perpetrator did forgo
This stress that is mentioned is the gift that just keeps on giving
Generationally it moves to the next and keeps on living
A voice was nonexistent but needed to temper the crime
Freedom is what was dreamt for and always stayed on the mind
Our heroes like Nat Turner and Sojourner Truth provided some glee
And gave people courage in attempting to flee
But now I am discovering that choice is what we have always had
It's the outcome of the options that has kept us scared and sad

Caressing Of A Soul

Loneliness I feel and I long for a touch
I implore you to caress as I need it that much
I am not sure how I got here without its behest
But I am realizing that my existence is unstable at best
If I don't start to thrive I will wither away
Understanding that all I did was to exist everyday
I know that in order to be touched you have to extend
But it seems like everyone has an agenda that leaves me on end
Sex is not the design but I will not out rightly reject
But the fondling of my soul is what I secretly expect
A genuine hug to help put me at ease
But subtle contact will do if you please
The cradling of my head sets my soul afire
But the electricity of a hand hold is also a desire
I need the tender handling of my fragile heart
Something I never received not even from the start
From a mother the gentle tenderness that I never had
The firm touch that I still yearn for from a fervent dad
The circumstances surrounding my introduction to others
Leaves me longing to relive the touch that a first date has to offer
Even a virtuous touch would help me to deal
A baby's small hand contacts deeply and compels you to feel
What about the metaphorical touch of a smile or a nod
Or the warm snuggle or wet nuzzle of a cat or a dog
I need gentleness that will make my soul come alive
Please touch me, because that is the only way I survive

A Warrior's Atonement

This may seem like I am once again scorning you
Today I am not completely sure what else to do
Why not in person you may ask
I either cannot find or am too embarrassed of this task
I write this now to right my wrong
I dealt you a blow from so very long
Ago, with a heartfelt sorry I give
I hope you understand and can now forgive
I didn't comprehend the depth of my sickness and my control
So my shortcomings that have since been revealed, I just didn't know
I am not blaming, the responsibility has been taken
I am just sad that you and our time together I have forsaken
You know who you are and you know what I owe
How sorry I am, I need you to know

Hope emerges

I Will Never Be The Same

It never dawned on me when I walked into the room
The same for which I was, was destined for doom
As I walked into the space with my heart heavy sighing
I saw people cheerful and laughing and I saw some that were crying
This spot I entered was a wonder to me
Some place that I never thought I would be
But how could this exist without me ever knowing
A place that could truly help, my mind was blowing
Smiles were freely given and even many a hug
Honestly, I was put aback, and my shoulders did shrug
Love from the entrance was given to me
But belief I deserved, dogged and eluded thee
They said that they would love and accept no matter what
They just wanted my acceptance as they already accepted me such
This initiated tears like I have never before
But like I would have in the past, I did not run for the door
I stayed to hear what more they had to say
And then like they asked, I came back another day
The folks in this room have seen me weep more than any other
These people now, I consider sisters and brothers
So, back and back continue I came
I realize now that I will never be the same

THE RE-BIRTH OF THE PHOENIX

It once was majestic as the last nail was driven
But the years have taken its toll and have not forgiven
Broken shutters, saggy roof, and paint that is worn
The journey for this old house has been incredibly long
An eyesore to all and not a good thing to say
This house is dilapidated on this very day
There is some fear for uncovering the unknown
Will the entirety need to be destroyed before regrown
Dry rot, termites, or other events to deal
These incidences will be discovered as the skin is peeled
Is it better to leave well enough alone
Or should this horrendous journey be taken on
But somebody had the vision of the grandeur of yore
So a chance was taken that there was good in the core
But a major demolition must be elect
In order for the new magnificence to stand erect
Tearing all the way down to the emotional core
To ensure longevity this must be done and more
Once exposed all of the acquired flaws
Now He can carefully lay and build all the walls
This new house is beginning to take a stately shape
Faith in the direction is what one must take
Some won't be able to comprehend what the process has in store
Others will be hopeful that it will be even better than before

Setbacks will come as the weather changes flight
But the ultimate goal is what will be kept in sight
As the furious construction continues to take place
The boldness of the lines begin to take shape
You thought it was grandiose in its hey
You should see it now in full splendor today
This old house on the street all did despise
Out of the ashes the mighty phoenix does arise

ONLY THE SHADOW KNOWS

My residence in the shadows has been eternally long
I was compelled into this so I could never be wrong
Ordered not to speak on things that didn't make sense
Sneaking around with the girlfriend when no match in our hints
Told I was too much and to tone it down
Joy had to be curtailed as I shifted into a frown
But how is it that Sharper can be so happy
I was dazed and perplexed as I couldn't see
Why can't I seem to enjoy like him I wonder
So through life I plod and I blunder
But the light has been shown and on me I must dote
I need to concentrate on my happiness as I have once wrote
Only I, my happiness I am responsible you see
Only then, out of the shadows, come will me

The Judgement Of Torture

I have shed my armor and now exposed
The rush of feeling is ever untold
Fear no longer begets the shield you see
But now it identifies real emotion in me
These sensations cut me deep to the bone
I am tortured now that I stand all alone
But the only way to get where I need to be
Is to be stripped to the core so that I can now see
Compassion to feel for all mankind
Understanding now that not all are blind
Forgiveness is something that I never had
A sentiment now that keeps me eternally clad
Judgement via the cover of the book
The dignity to decide their personal look
These observations, they are all new to me
For I am not sure how to currently see
The rush of emotion is difficult to handle
For now, I will sit in silence as I dance with the candle

I Got You

The best I try to be in anything I embark
But I must admit with fatherhood I truly missed the mark
I don't blame anyone for the faults that I have
I just wish I had the knowledge that I now do have
I wasn't nearly the best that sure is true
But you can best believe that I have always loved you
Not sure who can say they were the best but I wish I had known
Because I would have followed their lead way before you were grown
But I think you knew then and hope you still do
That through all my faults, I got you
When you were born and only my voice would settle you
You knew from the start that daddy got you
You would jump in the pool all carefree
Because you always knew that daddy has me
You dove off of the staircase with joy and glee
Because you knew without a doubt that daddy got me
When a stranger tried to talk to you and I roared, flee
It was confirmed to you that daddy got me
When you came on out and it didn't matter to me
Once again you knew that daddy got me
Today my presence is much more obscure
But your need for guidance and help continues to endure
I now stay in the background and let you do you
But always know that daddy got you

A Warriors Wish

I understand now that never met were my needs
But I could count on the giving of the physical deeds
Lights always on, mortgage paid right
I never had to worry about fleeing in the night
But I had to scrap for an emotional place in this land
In touch with my feelings I did not understand
As a result, a warrior I did become
Slaying all before me and then some
But whom does a gladiator come to rely
Although not ideal, it was my father, who died
In retrospect, I do seem to remember
Those early evil mornings of that late September
While biking and acting as the hood news hub
To ensure safe return, you shadowed your cub
Fast forward to those early hospital days
Where I was looked upon to make choices in a haze
No one remembers this onus put on me
But this is what a gladiator takes on you see
And no one knows that I whispered, "it's time to let go"
As I watched you slip away on that late night long ago
During this course, there was no sobbing or tears
There were objectives to slay and no time for fears
Funeral arrangements to make, family to arrive
I was raised to take all this and more in stride

Understanding the frugality of you over time
I changed the date to match your paradigm
But what about me, I wasn't allowed to grieve
I now had to take on all your responsibility
Making sure everyone else was ok
Again, able to do this because this is the gladiators way
But now years later, I sit and I mourn
Feelings are crashing and I am visibly torn
Not only do I bemoan for the childhood lost
I lament for him whose youth too had a cost
I understand now that you did the best you could
I only wish I could have better understood
But I was just a boy and needed you more
I needed rescue from those emotions that lay in store
I have felt eternally lost and oh so alone
Even more so now that you are all gone
My compass seems to be always askew
So harrowing that I never seem to know what to do
I need advice that only a father can give
My wish, is that god would have given you a few more to live

THE PATIENCE OF THE WAIT

I actually thought I knew what love was before
But I understand now that it was control in store
Retribution I would impose if you dared me
For however long I felt that it necessary
For a lifetime my head was in a space that I never understood
He, then graced me with his presence and it was all good
What was whispered to me that very lonely and teary night
If you are to recover, then patience must be in sight
He waited until the time I was ready to heal
But I resisted the guidance and was not able to deal
He waited until I gained the knowledge of the steps
But I was still confused and my feelings were bereft
He waited until I had the courage to make amends
Indicating that healing was just around the bend
He waited until I peeled the onion of hidden feelings
Emotions were stirring and I could tell I was healing
He then led me down the path of connected eternity
Revealing how amazing that perseverance could be
This patience that was exposed was a measurement of my faith
So amazing the journey, it was worth the wait

THE WARRIOR CHILD

What is it worth, the child's soul
Much more than any love you can dole
It's much too precious to assign a price to
But we as adults…do what we do
We parent consistent with our cultural assignment
Not accounting for our own conscious message alignment
Embarrassed because others may deem them wild
Ascribing greater value than those of the child
But what is the detriment to this precious little soul
I'll tell you what some sacrificed in the days of old
The consumption of evil is the price that we pay
Abandonment and embarrassment is the result of this foray
Remembering the dimming of the light in their eye
Causes this former gladiator to break down and cry
The tattering of the spirit is a huge expense
The task of healing is equally immense
Doesn't matter what people have to say
Be strong and model in your own special way
Who cares how many times they need to be told
Keep articulating until the story unfolds
They are pliable and we need to constantly teach
Not scold and spank and keep out of reach

So lay down your sword and be happy and free
For this young warrior unequivocally needs you to be
If you don't, the child's soul will forever be lost
I, for one, am no longer willing to pay that cost

UNDER THE ARMOR

Frivolity Of Life

What is life, I don't know but it is meant to be enjoyed
Meaning more significantly than where we are employed
This space should not be taken so seriously
So, go on out and fucking play roller derby
Skydive if you want or walk barefoot in the park
Go to the beach at night or catch a glimpse of a spark
California sunshine is meant to be enjoyed
I remember phenomenal times when I was a boy
Emulating Evil Knievel and jumping the cans
Erecting forts and digging ditches on anybody's land
If you don't go to the beach often then why would you stay
California lifestyle craves the necessity to play
There are festivals to cherish like the garlic and more
There is even the state fair for all to adore
Napa Valley is famous but we have much more wine
Try Lodi, Livermore or Santa Barbara next time
Music to listen and events to attend
Even roads that are begging for your whip to bend
Kayaking, scuba diving, maybe flying a kite
How about taking a road trip late at night
Forget about being house poor or leveraging the funds
You must preserve the nest egg if you are to discover what's fun
The latest gadget will not bring you lifelong glee
Only experiences will bring the joy you so desperately need

So leave your comfort zone and see what life has to offer
Next time someone asks what do you, work is not the proffer
You see I am a father, a poet, a significant other
A friend, son, an uncle and a brother
My vocation is not any more significant than these
So let's say what you do for real if you please
The world is my canvas, an artist at heart
We should be working to play, not working to start
We oft think our desires are wrong and out of reach
So do something courageous like walk nude on a beach

MY HERO

A hero is defined as a person that who,
In the face of adversity would still sacrifice to save you
They would combat hardships using impressive feats of strength
Often yielding themselves to go to these great lengths
Dr. King, now he embodied this true definition
Surrendering his own life for the ultimate mission
What about Malcom and the way his character leaned
Necessary for the cause by any means
Sometimes it's those hidden figures that work behind the scenes
Sacrificing for the greatness of all human beings
By the way, you are not a hero unless something heroic you do
And you are not a hero, unless someone else deems you
So to that I say, I dub my ABC with hero status
Doing everything he could to ensure AK matters
Sacrificing it all to guarantee he got into college
Completely understanding the ultimate necessity for this knowledge
Forgoing health, career, and sometimes even pay
Now that is the true definition of a hero in this modern day
But not to worry, the fruits of this labor will reveal themselves soon
Because one day near we all call AK, Dr. Spoon!

The Heart Of The Artist

Mining their world to express to you
To the depths of their soul to do what they do
Word choice, paint choice or canvas and such
Leaves the observer to interpret the handiwork much
Their innermost convictions that they choose to share
They are fully exposing their raw emotions out there

You would not believe all the art that goes unshared
Or those that continue to be unfinished wares
A deliberate chaos is what the artist has in mind
As they construct their creation one piece at a time

The intimate internal workings of their brain and heart
Their hurts, their triumphs, that have come from the start
No matter what the medium is of choice
It can be acted, written or using the voice

For you, the individual, to like is not the goal
But rather to reach that one wanting soul
For that very exact moment this piece they crave
Their soul touching yours like the whip to a slave

Understanding by some, but not by all
Their passion expressed spring, summer, winter, and fall
Into the project, their soul an artist painstakingly puts

All for that one chance to share their most intimate what's

Their latest creation, be careful to denounce
As they have crawled into the abyss to glean and announce
Creating art is tapping into a much greater feel
As they too have a story from which to heal

Old School Ballers

How did we get here and where are we going
We have traversed much ground without even knowing
Remember the Record Tree, Anderson Bros and the Alley of Alpine
Playing pinball, video games and other cool lines
Cruising on our ten speeds then rolling in cars
Seem like only yesterday we were walking the streets of the Gards
That's VGS to all my Mexican homies
Back then we were all one big family
House parties, school dances it all is a blur
Remember we called them brunches at Goethe my sir
Rolling in the Pontiac bumping Cutie Pie and That Girl
Boy those times sure where a whirl
Lucky, LB, GV, and my Goethe crew
Cannot believe we survived and all of us grew
Now we are all responsible fathers
Watching over this brand new breed of ballers
How could we see where we would be today
Can't believe 50 is what we now say
Where did all the time go my friend
Old School Ballers until the very end.

SHE IN THE FLOWERED DRESS

The caress of your dress to the curve of your hip
Your eyes shine of a happy sadness

Your smile explodes like a volcano erupt
As you conversate effortlessly you stand abrupt

As the pink flowers cling to your sinful frame
Your hair cascades like a daunting rain

This happy sadness of which I speak
There is a story there that all must seek

Beauty on the street corner
Who would have thought

A chance encounter
Of which was caught.

CUDDLE WEATHER

The sky is dark, ground is wet, and the air is damp and cold
The wind is such that the chill cuts through you so bold
The trees they are a swaying on this very blistery day
To be with you is truly what is on my mind this way
Yet we must trudge ourselves into it for our nine to five
But getting home to you is what makes my mind thrive
Visions of sitting with you on the couch, a fire and a glass of wine
This is the perfect end of this kind of day for which to unwind
Where are you my love, have you forsaken thee
This weather today was made just for you and me

STYLE AND GRACE

Whatever happened to charm, elegance and class
The images of today have a women's youth yearning to last
A recently viewed feature titled Mothers and Daughters
Envisioned thoughts of why one would decide to maim and slaughter
The beauty that was provided to them from above
Yet so fleeting like that the span of a dove
Filling their bodies with Botox, collagen, saline or whatever
Let's be like the lovely Selma Blair and keep it together
Women hitherto let the aging process proceed with glee
Understanding that gents would still awe in their beauty
To puff up the lips is a cause for jest
Further deciding to augment the breast
Or the ridiculous habit of increasing the hips
Talking about fake, man ain't that a blip
Hold onto what god gave you and for that you will find
The lid that compliments the pot and it will be kind
Right now he is looking, watching and waiting to see
Hoping and praying to get the opportunity
To alter would be cruel and leave him a bust
Because now the lid does not match the pot he did trust
He will love you with the mosquitoes, thin lips or flat
Or with mounds, full lips, and baby with back
It is you that he seeks, not the superficial wares
Because as he ages he will not know what to do with the fares

But caring and love will endure for a life
And that is really what he seeks when selecting a wife
I implore you to be like Sophia (Loren), Salma
(Hayek), Sandra (Oh), or, Halle (Berry)
They have aged with grace and are still as lovely as can be
You say hey, but these are stars that can afford the potentials
Including Facials, Pilates, and all the essentials
Well let me introduce you to some of my Facebook Friends
All I have known for decades and will till the very end
There's Kuwa, Darla, Alina, and especially the Rib
They all are incredible beauties and never once over did
So I guess the profound story I am trying to tell
Is please let us appreciate all you that is real
Although the media will continue to lie to your face
I beg of you to let yourself age with style and grace

Savoring The Encounter

While walking through life I could detect no fun
But events I embark seem like there should be some
Trips, vacations, parties and things
But I never seemed to hear the happy bell ring
I have not had anything lasting to trust
So they seemed unreal and destined to bust
No one told me I was supposed to enjoy
How often could they have when I was a boy
My trust in a higher power now helps me to see
The things I really want to make me happy
My boys to hang, hot springs to dip
Even to the beach on a surfing trip
Barefoot in the park, flying a kite
Commanding a drone or riding a bike
Pushing the whip, retirement too
Accomplishing the things I really want to
Writing a book accelerates my chi
Envisioning the possibility for all to see
My walk through life is now a run
Today I am constantly sprinting towards fun
These occasions I mention bring me pure joy
I can no longer manage others attempts to destroy

HIS PURPLENESS

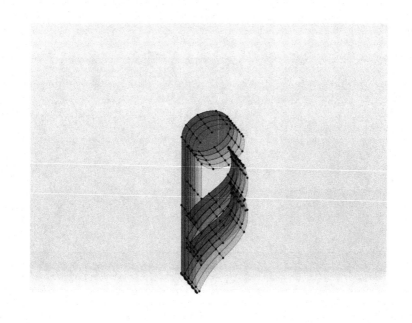

Purple Reign

With me at the brunches, house parties, and even Das Club

Honoring this Prince among men is serious cause to pop bub

His Royalness was definitely way ahead of his time

Penning stories like <u>Darling Nikki</u>, <u>Lady Cab Driver</u>, and <u>Black Sweat</u>
during his prime

How his individuality touched so many during his reign supreme

This icon was a gracious and generous human being

Helping so many like Morris Day and the Time

You won't believe the titles included in his rhymes

Concerts of Purple Rain, Musicology, Hit and Run and Jam of the Year

Makes me wonder if there can be a more prolific concerteer

From day one, <u>controversy</u> is what caused women to stop

Wearing puffy shirts, make-up and sometimes even naked from the top

<u>Insatiable</u> is what we would call his appetite for music you see

And whenever he got on one, <u>Soft and Wet</u> was she

Vanity, Apollonia, and Mayte were part of his clan

Let's just say he had some of the finest women in the land

Cruising in the Ponti rocking <u>DMSR</u> and <u>Head</u> as some of the faves.

Now rolling in the Tesla and still bumping these raves.

I was half a score plus three, when this majestic journey began

But your virtuosity was cut short and could not finish the span

Good night and God bless to you, my innovatively dressed purple friend

Your music will endure and be with me until my dying end

ABOUT THE AUTHOR

Brian Coates was born and raised in Sacramento, California. He was 10 years old when divorce struck his family. He then lived with his father for the next 10 years. Having survived childhood, Brian is currently on a journey of recovery. During this journey he has discovered poetry as a way to communicate his pain, his discovery, and his recovery.